AF228465

OUTDOOR ADVENTURES

ARCHERY

By Kelly Anne White

CONTENT CONSULTANT

Dana Keller
Level 3 USA Archery Instructor

SportsZone

An Imprint of Abdo Publishing
abdobooks.com

abdobooks.com

Published by Abdo Publishing, a division of ABDO, PO Box 398166, Minneapolis, Minnesota 55439. Copyright © 2020 by Abdo Consulting Group, Inc. International copyrights reserved in all countries. No part of this book may be reproduced in any form without written permission from the publisher. SportsZone™ is a trademark and logo of Abdo Publishing.

Printed in China
092019
012020

Cover Photo: iStockphoto
Interior Photos: iStockphoto, 5, 6, 22, 25, 27, 33, 34, 39; S&G/Press Association/AP Images, 8–9; Shutterstock Images, 11, 14, 30, 43; Elena Zakh/Shutterstock Images, 13; Maxim Mayorov/Shutterstock Images, 17; Susan Schmitz/Shutterstock Images, 18; Andrew Linscott/iStockphoto, 21; Marcel Jancovic/Shutterstock Images, 29; Dean Alberga/World Archery Federation/Getty Images Sport/Getty Images, 37; Koki Yamada/Shutterstock Images, 40; Vince Talotta/Toronto Star/Getty Images, 44

Editor: Patrick Donnelly
Series Designer: Colleen McLaren

Library of Congress Control Number: 2019941980

Publisher's Cataloging-in-Publication Data

Names: White, Kelly Anne, author
Title: Archery / by Kelly Anne White
Description: Minneapolis, Minnesota : Abdo Publishing, 2020 | Series: Outdoor adventures | Includes online resources and index
Identifiers: ISBN 9781532190452 (lib. bdg.) | ISBN 9781532176302 (ebook)
Subjects: LCSH: Archery--Juvenile literature. | Bow and arrow--Juvenile literature. | Targets (Sports)--Juvenile literature. | Outdoor recreation--Juvenile literature. | Sports--Juvenile literature.
Classification: DDC 799.32--dc23

TABLE OF CONTENTS

CHAPTER 1

THE GAME IS TO AIM

It's an outdoor woodland adventure. The archer has a bow and arrow at the ready. He treads lightly along the wooded trail. He stealthily peers around a tree. And there it is: a majestic elk! The archer raises his bow and shoots. The point of the arrow plunges into the animal. But the elk does not fall or run. The archer walks over and pulls out the arrow. The elk is still standing because it's not a real animal. It is a three-dimensional (3-D) model, positioned for target practice.

The goal in archery is to hit the center of a target with an arrow shot from a bow. Some archers shoot

A bowhunter enjoys a breathtaking view.

Archery ranges feature targets set up in lanes.

strictly for marksmanship. Others are wild-game hunters. Either way, archery is a popular activity.

Target archery involves shooting at stationary targets from set distances. Standard targets have 10 rings in five colors. Just like a bowling alley has

lanes, target archery ranges usually have shooting
lanes. Some people begin by taking classes indoors.
Indoor archery ranges are ideal during rainy or cold
seasons. Moving to outdoor shooting lanes brings
challenges such as wind and other environmental
conditions. But outdoor archery has its benefits, such
as fresh air, sunshine, and birdsong.

Field archery is done on outdoor courses that can
be hilly, unlike usually flat target ranges. Archers
hike along trails or in fields. They are on a quest for
multiple targets that are posted at various points
along the way. Some archery courses use life-size
3-D animals. The fake animals are made of solid
foam. The animals can be placed around bends,
hidden in coves, or positioned behind greenery. This
is to sharpen the senses of the archers, who shoot at
the fakes as they spot them.

MEET AND COMPETE

Archers often meet up for friendly competition.
Archery clubs host area events and classes.

Archery was featured at the 1908 Olympic Games in London.

They offer lessons for archers of all skill
levels. Archers take part in local competitions.
Larger organizations oversee national and
global championships.

Archery is a world-class sport. It became part
of the Olympic Games in 1900. In 1904 women
competed. It was one of the first Olympic sports
to welcome female competitors. One of the best

ARCHERY'S HISTORY

Archery has been around since ancient times. Evidence of it has been discovered all over the world. It was used primarily for hunting and combat. It likely started in the Stone Age. In the late 1700s, archery shifted from a survival skill to more of a recreational activity for well-to-do Europeans. That's because technological advances led to the invention of more sophisticated weapons used for survival purposes. Many indigenous peoples throughout the world continue to rely on bowhunting today.

female archers of all time is Kim Soo-Nyung of South Korea. She earned four gold medals, one silver, and a bronze between 1988 and 2000. "Archery gives you conviction," she says.

The most decorated archer in Olympic history is Hubert van Innis. The Belgian won six Olympic gold medals and three silvers between 1900 and 1920. After that, archery was cut from the Olympics. But it made its comeback in 1972 and has been part of the Olympics ever since. Archery is also featured in the Junior Olympics.

Para archery is included in the Paralympic Games. Para archery is for athletes with physical disabilities.

Para archery makes the sport accessible to athletes who use wheelchairs.

Para archery was introduced in England in 1948 as an exercise for injured military veterans. Many para archery competitions are now held around the world.

Archery is taken seriously as a competitive sport. Archery competitions often involve many official committees, directors, deputies, scorers, and commissions. But it also can be an informal recreational activity. Many archers shoot just for fun.

GETTING IN GEAR

Archery requires, of course, a bow and some arrows. But archers can choose from several types of bows. Arrows also come in different varieties. Other equipment is necessary as well. Gearing up means making a few important decisions.

CHOOSING A BOW

Selecting the right bow depends on many factors. Will the bow be used for competition or recreation? How strong and how skilled is the archer? The archer's height and draw length determine the correct size of the bow. There are three bows that are most commonly used in archery.

The longbow is known for its simplicity. It's made from a basic piece of curved wood. Because it's

The ends of a recurve bow curve back away from the archer.

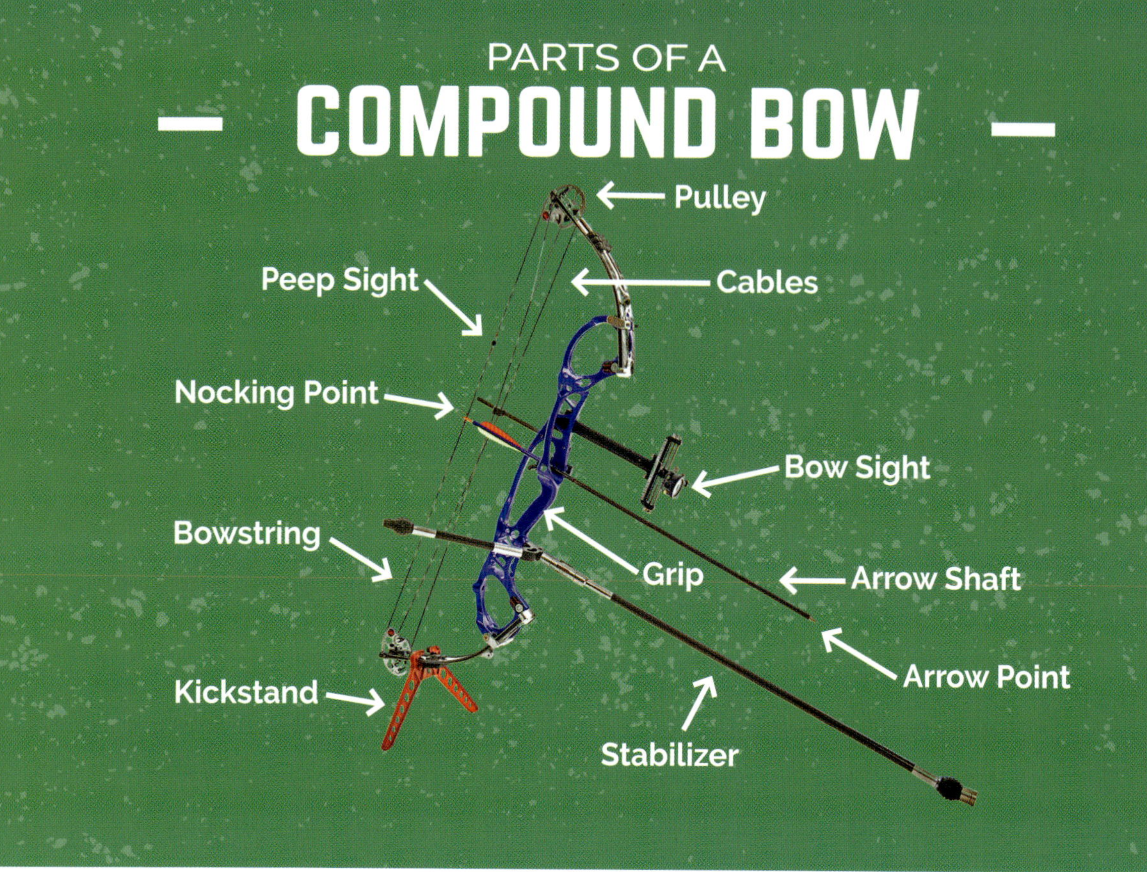

inexpensive, the longbow can be a good starter bow. Like all other bows, it has a handle at its center. Most bows also have an arrow rest above the handle grip. This is to keep the arrow steady until it leaves the bow. The parts of the bow on either side of the handle are called limbs. Notches at the ends of both limbs hold the bowstring. Just as its name suggests, the longbow is very long. It is often close to the same height as the archer.

The recurve bow also lives up to its name. Both ends of the wood curve back, so the bow has a bit of a curly look to it. This design gives the bow its power. The recurve bow is often made of fiberglass and other synthetic materials, but some are wooden. The handle is usually aluminum alloy or wood. This is the only type of bow permitted in Olympic competition.

The compound bow has an off-center pulley on the end of each limb. These pulleys manage a system of cables and bowstring. The system makes it easier for the archer to pull back the bowstring. It also provides extra thrust, making the arrows travel much faster. Some archers feel this is the easiest bow to manage.

TIME TO ACCESSORIZE

A bow is the most basic piece of archery equipment. But without a few other accessories, an archery bow isn't terribly useful.

Arrows come in many different styles and sizes. The arrows' thickness and length must match the bow's weight and length. The body of an arrow is its shaft, and the sharp tip is the point. Archers can choose from many different kinds of arrow points as well. The groove fitted into the spot where the arrow meets the string is known as the nock. Fletchings are attached just below the nock to help the arrow spin when it is in flight. Fletchings can be either individual strips of plastic called feathers or single pieces of plastic called vanes.

A quiver is a protective holder for the archer's arrows. Some quivers are cases with straps that make them easier for the archer to carry. Others can be attached to the hip or set on the ground. Many newer recurve and compound bows have quivers that attach to the bows.

These arrows have vanes and are being held in a quiver.

String literally ties the bow together. Bowstring comes in lots of colors, even bright neon and multicolored rainbow hues. Two types of string are used for longbows and recurve bows: Flemish twist and endless loop. Both types have some braiding. Compound bows use one main bowstring and one or more cables.

Targets at archery clubs and ranges come in a variety of sizes and styles, too. Some are paper targets attached to heavy foam blocks or bales made of wood and wool. Many field ranges have 3-D animal targets. These are also made of foam. On private land, archers sometimes make their own targets. Targets can be made of tough plastic trash bags or large burlap sacks. The bags can be stuffed with old clothing, rubber tire pieces, or other material. Some archers like to paint bull's-eyes on the fronts of the sacks.

Safety and comfort are important, so some archers wear a leather or plastic guard on the arm that holds the bow. It protects the arm from being scraped or hit by the arrow or bowstring. Some archers also wear a leather glove. Archery gloves don't come in pairs, and they have only three fingers. They go over the first three fingers of the hand that pulls back the bowstring. The glove makes for a smoother release. It also protects the fingers from friction.

A young archer aims at a 3-D model of a deer.

CHAPTER 3

SAFE, NOT SORRY

Safety is a huge factor in archery. On archery ranges, both spectators and archers need to stay alert and safe. Archery ranges have multiple rules that archers and spectators must follow.

Safe archery practice means well-kept equipment. It means routine equipment inspections, too. A bow should be thoroughly checked before and after shooting. It also should be wiped with a clean, dry cloth. Archers must watch for twists, cracks, and weak spots in bows. Problems such as broken grips and loose bolts can be unsafe as well.

Other equipment issues can be safety factors in archery. Bows and arrows need to be appropriately sized to the archer. The bowstring must be strong

Inspecting your equipment is an important part of safety at the range.

Arrows with frayed or damaged fletchings should be replaced.

and not frayed. An incorrectly placed peep sight can cause an archer's aim to be off. And regardless of equipment, children and beginners should have a skilled instructor.

AWAY WITH STRAY ARROWS

Arrows should also be inspected before shooting. Archers look down the length of the arrow to check for crookedness. Crooked or cracked arrows are unsafe. Arrows with broken nocks or loose fletchings aren't safe either. They all can lead the arrow to go astray and not hit its intended target.

Archers need to practice safety when shooting an arrow. The arrow is nocked when it is fitted onto the bowstring before a shot. Nocked arrows should always be pointed toward the ground until the archer is ready to shoot. Arrows should never be shot straight up into the air. Also, archers should not shoot at other archers' targets. Archery clubs and ranges typically have strict safety guidelines posted.

WHAT NOT TO WEAR

Archers don't need to be stylish. But they do have to wear proper attire. Most archers dress for comfort and weather conditions. But they should avoid loose clothing. Baggy sleeves and dangling jewelry might get tangled up in the bowstring. Long hair should be tied back, too.

It's important for archers and spectators to follow all safety rules.

Targets that are too small or too thin to stop an arrow should not be used. And shooting at solid objects, such as cinder blocks, is dangerous because arrows might bounce off them and hit someone. When an archer is shooting, no one should stand within 50 yards (45 m) of any side of the target.

Of course, it's impossible to steer clear of a target when retrieving an arrow. To retrieve an arrow, an archer must be certain no other archers are at the shooting line. Safe archery ranges always have shooting lines. These establish a safe distance for shooting. They also provide a visual boundary for archers and spectators. Arrows should be pulled out one at a time. One hand is held flat against the target. The other hand pulls out the arrow. Archers must also be careful to pick up arrows that are on or in the ground. When not in use, arrows should always be stored securely in a quiver.

Archers need to be cautious when retrieving arrows.

An injury can put a damper on the fun of any sport. Archery is no exception. Anyone taking up archery, whether as a serious sport or just for fun, needs to know its important safety rules.

CHAPTER 4

SKILLS AND TECHNIQUES

Archery is not a one-size-fits-all sport. There are various methods of shooting an arrow. An archer's dominant eye determines which hand to use. Right-handed archers typically hold the bow in the left hand and draw the bowstring with the right. Left-handed archers do the opposite.

GETTING A GRIP

Archers should keep a relaxed grip on the bow's handle. The grip should be set in the part of the hand between the thumb and index finger. The thumb

An archer's grip on the bow should be relaxed and comfortable.

should point at the target, while the other fingers relax and wrap around the grip.

For the hand that pulls the bowstring, finger positions are key. The fingers do not touch the arrow. They touch only the string. Archers pull the string with three fingers. They use the index finger, middle finger, and ring finger. They can choose from two finger positions for the bowstring hand. The three-under position places all three fingers on the bowstring under the nock of the arrow. With the split-finger position, the index finger is above the nock of the arrow. The other two fingers are below the nock.

TAKING A STANCE

Before shooting, archers must first get in the proper stance. Posture matters, and so does foot placement.

— STEPPING IT UP —

Archery is a step-by-step procedure. Its actions take place in a sequence of events. This is true regardless of what type of bow is used. Once an archer takes a stance, the proper sequence is as follows:

1. Nock—Secure the back of the arrow to the bowstring and its shaft on the bow's arrow rest.

2. Set—Place one hand around the grip of the bow and the fingers of the other hand on the bowstring.

3. Set up—Raise the bow and arrow in preparation for a shot.

4. Draw—Pull the bowstring back toward the side of the face.

5. Anchor—Pull the string back until the tip of the index finger touches the corner of the mouth.

6. Hold—Steady the anchor by engaging the back muscles and locking the bow arm in place.

7. Aim—Align the peep sight and sight housing and gauge the distance to the target.

AURORA

A centered body makes a solid position from which to shoot. An unstable stance could send an arrow way off target. In a basic stance, the feet straddle the shooting line. Then the archer pivots the upper body toward the target to shoot.

Once the archer releases the bowstring, it's important to keep follow-through in mind. Archers should keep their arms steady after the release so the arrow starts out on a straight trajectory. Any subtle movement can send the arrow flying off course.

An experienced archer completes the archery steps fluidly. The archer must focus on the target while maintaining form. Perfect form in archery is known as T-form. Proficient archery takes plenty of practice.

Proper follow-through gives the arrow a better chance to fly straight.

CHAPTER 5

POINTING OUT THE RULES

Like most sports, archery can be done just for fun. But it also can be an organized event. Either way, archers can take part in many different games. Tournaments are held indoors or outdoors. Archers might compete individually or in teams. Typically in a competition, the shooting takes place from a set distance ranging from 30 to 90 meters. Archers each shoot a certain number of arrows in a series of rounds. Each arrow that hits the target earns a score. The score depends on which part of the target is hit.

Archery is a sport that can take place indoors or outdoors.

Colored rings on the target help archers determine their score.

KEEPING SCORE

Scores are based on the colored rings around an
archery target. Scores are usually determined after

an archer has shot several arrows. Customarily the archer shoots six arrows from a long distance and three arrows from a shorter distance. Then the archer calls out his or her own score. Other archers verify the accuracy of the score. Archers are not allowed to touch the target or its arrows until scores are verified.

The goal is to hit inside the center circle. That is worth the most points. Outer circles are worth fewer points. When an arrow hits the line that separates two colors on the target, the higher score is applied. An arrow that does not stick to the target earns a score only if it leaves a mark. If an arrow sticks into the nock of another arrow in the target, it scores the same as the first arrow. And arrows that bounce from the ground and then hit the target do not earn any points.

If an archer drops an arrow, the archer gets a second chance to shoot that arrow. But that applies only if the archer can reach the arrow from the shooting line. If the archer has to step over the shooting line to pick up the arrow, it scores a zero.

ARCHERY'S HIERARCHIES

Many associations oversee organized archery events. They also govern the formal rules of the sport. Separate agencies are in place to sanction professional and amateur archers, bowhunters, archery in schools, and Olympic and Paralympic archers around the world. Several have local chapters as well. Each of them serves a unique purpose.

For example, World Archery is the international organization that governs archery as a sport. It is based in Switzerland. Its mission is to regulate archery worldwide. The World Archery federation used to be known as the Fédération Internationale de Tir à l'Arc (FITA).

Most archery tournaments in the United States follow

An archer from the Netherlands competes in the 2019 Archery World Cup in Antalya, Turkey.

the same format. The first round is based on FITA rules. This is followed by a round formatted after the Olympics. A FITA round consists of 144 total arrows shot. The Olympic round involves a player elimination process.

CHAPTER 6

NEW SPINS ON AN OLD SPORT

Different activities involving archery have developed over time. Several are done just for recreation. Many are performed in competition. Some are variations on traditional target archery. Others combine field archery with various other sports.

In flight archery, archers shoot for distance only. No target is involved in this type of tournament. As with target archery, they start from a lane behind a shooting line. They simply shoot their arrows forward into the air. The goal is to shoot the arrow as far as possible. Scoring is determined by the distance of the arrow's flight.

Some traditional forms of archery are demonstrated at cultural fairs or festivals.

An archer participates in kyudo at a festival in Hokkaido, Japan.

Archery golf is a blend of two popular sports. The goal is to shoot arrows long distances down the fairway. Archers begin at the tee of each hole. Some archery golf courses have physical targets near each golf hole. Others simply require the arrow reach within a few feet of the hole. Sometimes archers make their own archery golf courses in fields or other open land.

Ski archery blends archery with cross-country skiing. It's similar to biathlon. Biathlon combines skiing and rifle shooting. In ski archery, the cross-country skier does not carry a rifle. Instead, the skier carries a bow and arrow in a backpack. The goal is to race through a snowy course. Targets are set up along the way. Ski archers shoot from a kneeling position. With each missed target, the archer must ski a penalty loop before continuing on the course.

An arcathlon event combines archery and running. Archers stop at specific spots to shoot at fixed targets. They shoot from a standing or kneeling position. The arcathlon track is usually five to 12 kilometers. Bows might be kept at each shooting spot. Otherwise, archers carry their bows while running.

TRADITIONAL FORMS

Kyudo means "the way of the bow" in Japanese. Kyudo treats archery as a martial art. It is considered a form of meditation. With kyudo, the bow and arrow are not meant to be used as weaponry. Instead, they are tools of spiritual development.

Kyudo uses a hit-or-miss scoring system. Kyudo is often competitive, but the primary goal is not to beat an opponent. The focus is on personal form and concentration. A kyudo bow is called a *yumi*. The arrow is a *ya*. Both are traditionally crafted of bamboo, hickory, or other native wood.

Horse archery is done on horseback. It is particularly challenging because the rider must let go of the reins. Some horse archers shoot at targets while mounted on a horse that's standing still. Others shoot while riding. Horse archery honors the archery of many cultures, such as the Korean, Hungarian, and Comanche cultures.

MODERN FUN

Archery tag is kind of like paintball or laser tag. Players form teams and try to shoot their opponents. Of course, players do not shoot one another with pointed arrows. They use special arrows with foam tips that look like marshmallows. Players also wear helmets for safety. Archery tag is played inside

An archer takes aim during a horse archery competition.

arenas or outside in fields. Players dodge arrows to avoid getting hit. Or, because nonlethal arrows are used, they can even catch them in their hands!

Most 3-D field archery courses use stationary targets. But in moving-target archery, field archers take aim at mobile targets such as mechanical animal figures. Some are mounted on wheels. Others move along tracks or travel on cables attached to

43

Archery tag has become popular with younger archers.

trees. Not all moving targets are 3-D animals. Some archers shoot at rolling soccer balls. Others shoot at swinging balls that hang from cords.

As with archery tag, hoverball archery uses foam-tipped arrows. The archer shoots at inflated balls that float above plastic cones. Forced air is emitted from the cones to make the balls hover. Hoverball archery requires purchasing or renting a fairly large piece of equipment. A square inflatable frame holds the cones. It hooks up to an electrical source for the airflow. It resembles a carnival game booth. Hoverball archery equipment is available for party rental in some areas.

Many other games are designed around archery. Archers make simple adjustments, such as attaching playing cards, inflated balloons, or cartoon cutouts to the target. At the World Nomad Games, which is dedicated to preserving historical and cultural sports in Central Asia, gymnasts even perform archery with their feet while doing handstands! The future points to archery evolving with even more challenging formats.

Three young archers aimed to become Brazil's first indigenous Olympic athletes. Nelson Silva, Graziela Paulino, and Dream Braga tried out for the 2016 Games in Rio de Janeiro. They were part of a project that aims to find world-class athletes among Brazil's indigenous population. None of them made the team. But Silva and Paulino teamed up to win a gold medal in a doubles event at the 2015 Brazilian national championship.

GLOSSARY

accessories
Objects that add effectiveness to something else.

alloy
A compound of two or more metals.

archer
A person who uses a bow and arrow.

bull's-eye
The center of a target.

cables
Fiber cord for the pulley system of a compound bow.

combat
Active fighting in a war.

fairway
The pathway between the tee and the green on a golf course.

fiberglass
A composite of glass in fibrous form.

marksmanship
Skill in shooting at a mark or target.

thrust
Forward movement.

trajectory
A line of progression.

MORE INFORMATION

BOOKS

Berg, Christian. *Archery from A to Z: An Introductory Guide to a Sport Everyone Can Enjoy.* Mechanicsburg, PA: Stackpole Books, 2019.

Marinas, Amante P., Sr. *Archery for Beginners: The Complete Guide to Shooting Recurve and Compound Bows.* North Clarendon, VT: Tuttle Publishing, 2019.

Nayeri, Daniel. *The Most Dangerous Book: An Illustrated Introduction to Archery.* New York: Workman Publishing, 2017.

ONLINE RESOURCES

To learn more about archery, please visit **abdobooklinks.com** or scan this QR code. These links are routinely monitored and updated to provide the most current information available.

INDEX

ABOUT THE AUTHOR

Kelly Anne White is an author of several books for kids, and she has edited hundreds of books in nearly every genre. Prior to her ventures into book publishing, White spent 15 years as executive editor of *Girls' Life* magazine. She is on staff at the central Enoch Pratt Free Library, and she conducts courses in professional studies at Morgan State University in Baltimore.